# The Raincoat Colors

*poems by*

# Helena Minton

*Finishing Line Press*
Georgetown, Kentucky

# The Raincoat Colors

Copyright © 2017 by Helena Minton
ISBN 978-1-63534-303-8 First Edition
All rights reserved under International and Pan-American Copyright Conventions.
No part of this book may be reproduced in any manner whatsoever without written permission from the publisher, except in the case of brief quotations embodied in critical articles and reviews.

## ACKNOWLEDGMENTS

Grateful acknowledgment is made to the following publications in which some of these poems, sometimes in different form, first appeared:

*Masspoetry.org*: "Dark Tasks, A Dream"
*Parting Gifts*: "The Letter Opener," "Interlude," "Lenses"
*Red River Review*: "Prescription"
*Renovation Journal*: "Habits"
*ROAR Magazine, A Journal of the Literary Arts by Women*: "Furnished Model"
*Route 9*: "Cascade"
*Solstice Literary Magazine: A Magazine of Diverse Voices*: "Thinking of the Anhinga"
*Sou'wester*: "Adamantine"
*The Tower Journal*: "The Garden Behind the Garden"

Thank you to my family and to my friends, especially to the evening workshop poets, whose advice helped shape many of these poems.


Publisher: Leah Maines

Editor: Christen Kincaid

Cover Art: "Seascape," Helen S. Minton

Author Photo: Edward M. De Innocentis

Cover Design: Elizabeth Maines McCleavy

Printed in the USA on acid-free paper.
Order online: www.finishinglinepress.com
　　　　　also available on amazon.com

Author inquiries and mail orders:
Finishing Line Press
P. O. Box 1626
Georgetown, Kentucky 40324
U. S. A.

# Table of Contents

Home Truths ..................................................................... 1
Habits ............................................................................... 3
Instant ............................................................................. 4
Impala .............................................................................. 5
The Dead Keep Us Company ........................................ 6
Lenses .............................................................................. 7
Dedication ...................................................................... 8
Hotel de L'Avenir ......................................................... 10
Luxembourg VIII ......................................................... 12
The Garden Behind the Garden .................................. 14
Wave, Night .................................................................. 15
Prescription .................................................................. 16
The Letter Opener ....................................................... 17
Interlude ....................................................................... 18
Cascade ......................................................................... 19
Neighbor ....................................................................... 20
Furnished Model .......................................................... 21
Adamantine .................................................................. 23
Thinking of the Anhinga ............................................. 24
Dark Tasks, A Dream ................................................... 26
Time Travel ................................................................... 28
Direction ....................................................................... 31
High Summer ............................................................... 32

# Home Truths

A family is a unit of measure.
I belong to one.

A child is asked to draw her family.
Some are close. Is yours?

A nuclear family is a unit of power.
At the dinner table one sibling

is weighed against another.
Someone sees herself as a buffer

at these meals but why
would she want to?

This is the clan irritant,
the one who likes to argue.

This one won't eat red food.
The middle one is the most social.

The father sits at the head of the table
and carves, a dilemma:

white meat or dark,
three children, two legs.

The youngest pipes up.
*Don't interrupt.*

The father does not always speak
in measured tones.

He gives the mother
a peck on the cheek.

A unit of measure is exclusive.
Dry quarts. Liquid quarts.

Quartz crystals for the radio
the father never built for the son.

Some units are rarely used
in a household, the *gill*, for instance, or the *ohm*.

*You've got to eat a peck of dirt*
*before you die*

my grandmother always said.
It was reassuring to hear.

The nuclear family is exclusive.
A good neighbor doesn't need to knock.

Pencil marks that measure the children
grow fainter every year.

**Habits**

Her father's big hands
yanked crabgrass.
She sat beside him,
small legs dangling,
her fingers in her mouth.

He told her as a boy at Mass
he flipped his hands
palms up, palms down
until his mother hissed,
"What's the matter,
got St. Vitus' Dance?"

A disease like a dance—
what kind was that?
a square dance
or a skater's:
crack the whip?

*Keep your fingers
out of your mouth.*

Was that her disease?
a kind of distress,
a distress like a dance.

Her hands snap off blossoms,
clutch a broom, a hairbrush,
smooth a forehead.
They fly to her lips.
She can't stop them.

**Instant**

The March morning
my father died
a hot wind of cinders blew.

A force took hold,
a shock. Conductivity
shot through a wire

sent my body back
to my son's birth,
a January night,

not as a memory
but as a surge
in my blood,

the match-tips
of my nerves.
Lineage lit up electric

with connection.
Arrival, departure
father, son.

Icy birth,
windy death,
collided head to toe.

**Impala**

The last time I saw my father
we drove to Anna Maria Island
in a light rain,
the red, rented Impala
smooth as Florida
(he was going to find out
what kind of animal it was.)

Coffee at a German café,
a stroll on the old pier
past the pelicans
balanced on pilings—
big feet and down-turned
waiting beaks.

*An old man's afternoon,*
he called it.
Nowhere we had to be.
Swirl of white
on gray waves,
sky the pebbled calm
of a Japanese garden.

I can't account for
how we passed the hours,
what we talked about,
enclosed in the car
(sleek as a grassland antelope,
pausing once to lift its head,
grazing, not racing)
the last time I saw my father.

## The Dead Keep Us Company

Now when we speak
they don't interrupt.

They let us win every argument
with nowhere to go,

nothing but time on their hands.
Our conspirators, they forgive

what we can't forgive ourselves,
that we didn't listen harder.

We can tell by their eyes
they have things to reveal.

We give ourselves over to them,
great organizers

of intimate information,
patient, letting us stand

at the counter
until we are ready to choose.

Off-hand, they tell us
what no one else
has the heart to.

**Lenses**

Drugstore reading glasses:
black print on white paper
she holds in her hands,
obsessive and comforting.

Her grandfather's pince nez,
the silver-plated opera glasses
stamped: "Made in occupied Japan."

3D colors that jump out
from comic book tree tops
where the eye grapples and spins.

The lorgnette, grannies and Ben Franklins,
the speckled Medicare frames.

Rosy lenses, infinite
extra pairs she keeps
to filter the anxieties.

20-20 yearning.
Hiding in plain sight.

The magnifying glass
slides out of the dictionary
for scrutiny of the elusive.

The squint. The glare.
Myopia and hindsight.

## Dedication
*Hotel des Invalides*

You had planned a trip to Paris
before you died. I'm here in your place,
as you asked, my rooms overlooking
Rodin's rose garden
and, beyond, a city in itself,
the *Hotel des Invalides*: gilt basilica, military museums,
veterans asleep in upper wings—
missing you and your knowledge of history.

\*

Napoleon's vault on a dias,
six coffins within coffins,
in the echoing rotunda.
I lean on the marble balustrade
and peer down, take it on faith,
inside, there was once
a husband and father.

\*

It was hard to imagine
exile on Elba as punishment,
the air softened with lavender,
hot August on the soles of my feet
as we climbed the steps to his villa
the summer I was sixteen.
We saw the view of the sea his eyes fell on,
his writing desk, his pen set down
as though he had just left the room.
Who visits the island where he died,
stony St. Helena?

\*

I wish I could show you
the watercolors soldiers painted,
wash of green and blue
in a schoolboy's notebook,
faint pencil marks underneath:
World War I skirmishes
in farm towns with names
that belie the facts, lyrical,
*Amiens, Champagne, Chemin des Dames,*
towns we once drove through, speaking
this language I only half remember.

\*

Down the *Invalides'* long blocks,
lined with cannons,
lies a tiny park where you took me
when we lived here in the '50s.
In a grove of chestnut trees,
a statue of Anatole France—
how the French revere their writers:
their names inscribed on street corners
to guide day-dreamy tourists.
I sit on a bench near a man who reads
as his daughter digs a leaf nest.
No one but you knows I'm here
in the shadow of the emperor.

## Hotel de L'Avenir,
### *Paris*

Early morning, still shamefully dark.
A mourning dove's troubling coo

too close to my pillow,
persistent, on the ledge.

Its private brooding swirls
a vocal *deshabille*.

It can't quite clear its throat.
Is that the bird that tried to fly in

when I opened the window last night?
Gray breast feathers,

wings almost batting my hand.
I slammed both sides of the glass,

turned the handle tight.
Five flights up, I can't

leave the window open wide.
Below lies the courtyard

without flowers or fountains,
only space for trash and brooms.

I will take my morning promenade
along the street I can't see

from this room,
among those who stride to work

or hold their children's hands
on the way to the school

I attended years ago.
On the narrow sidewalk

children on scooters just miss my legs.
They know how much room

they have to maneuver.
I'm distracted, my daydreaming

a danger to myself and others.
I pretend I still live here,

grown up yet a little girl,
playing hide and seek

in the arched doorway.
I don't do as I should—

stay in my room
until I hear the bell.

Even before the street quiets,
the sun appears, I walk

determined to merge with others
on the just-washed sidewalks.

## Luxembourg VIII
### *After a lithograph by Harold Altman*

Paris, late afternoon.
Two women walking.
They carry purses or shopping bags
away from sunlight
into the blue-gray graveled shadows.

The green trees close in. Green turns to black
beyond where the branches bend toward each other
over a handprint of sunlight.

I feel the relief of leaving the heat
but what am I stepping into?

Swings where my father pushed me
or I pumped myself, my legs pushing
higher and higher.

Fountains, reflecting pools,
and the *bateaux*
my brother sailed with sticks.

A block from the *jardins*, we lived in a small hotel
my mother tells me smelled of scalded milk.

A walk-up, the electricity kept going out
and the concierge shouted *Attention!*
I rode my red scooter in the courtyard.

This Paris, this park belong to the artist,
his own light and dark, shadow and brilliance,
as he plays with, rearranges Paris.

I can't, don't walk here, although
I can report the feeling of being alone
in this city, late in the afternoon,
when all the noise stops at once
as I turn a corner and enter a shaded *allee*,
eager for the luxury:

to go home and lie down for a minute,
before the evening begins
and extends into another day.

## The Garden Behind the Garden
### *At the Memorial for the Deported, Notre Dame, Paris*

*Parvis*: a garden enclosed behind a church.
*Parvis*, paradise, the same root.
Was there a fence around paradise, a wrought-iron gate
to be opened by a weighty key hanging
from an angel's belt?

Behind Notre Dame red roses grow along the Seine.
I never thought of paradise enclosed
but how else to keep Adam and Eve
from rattling the gate, trying to get back in?
This summer day groups of tourists are visiting Notre Dame
but here none but me and a homeless man, asleep in a torn coat.

A policeman climbs the stairs to your apartment.
He holds a key, yells,
*pack a suitcase and out, out, get to the station.*

I never went down the steps to see the dimly lit cells
with the deported poets' words inscribed on the walls.
It was 1962. I started to go down
but my family was in a hurry
or I thought it was closed.

Or was I scared?
I tell myself I can go down another time.
It will be there.

I can count on it.

**Wave, Night**
    *After a painting by Georgia O'Keeffe*

Was that a splash?

Someone slipping into the water
and swimming away,
stealth in the dead of night,
all surface calm now, the struggle
long over.

Yet something woke you.
You sat up suddenly.

Black, smooth as piano keys, the nocturne
a melody of the dark, a deceptive sound
of going deep, of being told to sink or swim.

The surface hard as piano keys,
you make no sound,
you want to bang your hands down,
your head against it,
and the sound of the nocturne
haunting, mournful.

Whose sadness flows out of the keys?
Yours or someone else's
become flotsam, a thing of the past.

The light is poised at the end of the black horizon,
a beacon you want to reach out to
past the green and purple roll of waves.

**Prescription**

On a scorched evening
under a full moon,
one lone swimmer in the bay.

It could be you
shoulders relaxed,
buoyed on the waves.

When you visit the sea
you turn into the person
you thought you were.

First dreams don't always come true
and second, subsequent dreams,
what becomes of them?

When you visit the sea
you remember you want to live there,
as though you'd misplaced a longing

and now you want it written down,
to set in motion a reversal,
to quell your disposition.

Sand, swells, horizon,
evening's salt air in your lungs.
Longing will be key.

**The Letter Opener**

I felt separate from all of you.
I went to work, came home,
knew a kind of luxury.

Unable to sweep, to rinse a saucer,
unable to write a to-do list
and so unable to think.

I'm not allowed to say
I miss my broken wrist
now that it's mended.

The sling is gone
that protected more than bone.
My whole body's thrown

off-kilter. I don't know
what to do with myself,
let loose, at loose ends,

this cloudy March.
Undone by the weight
of a letter and
the ivory letter opener.

**Interlude**

As if waking up after years asleep

I open the book of painters from the Pacific Northwest:
Mark Tobey, Guy Anderson, Morris Graves,

their somber inkblot bouquets, their grays.
Here's Anderson's little still life—tendrils and stem—
a marine blue vase,
a chair, perhaps a corner of his fishing shack
painted offhand, a jumble, where my afternoon expands

away from obligations.
Among these hues I breathe evenly for the first time in days,
admiring the ones whose dreams turned on turpentine, tobacco,
their lives contained in a few shades. Such serious men.
In the '40s they took the logging roads to paint from fire lookouts.

Heron-still the pages unfold
with their beige, brown, black,
the raincoat colors.

# Cascade

I wake up in a room with too many objects
tilting toward me: books, lamps, stacks of paper.

A world with countless things, how to make sense of it?
Some collect coins or orchids, depression glass,
many of one.

Bravery of those who wade into the swamp
in search of the rarest shoot,

diligence of the woman who found
200 sand dollars one morning on the beach,
insisting on perfection,
no broken edge.

Collecting shows signs of genius
my father said once, or more than once,
enough so that I haven't forgotten it,

and he used to talk, too, of collections that tip toward madness,
the Collyer brothers' stacks of newspapers
serpentined along their hallways.
Now it is a condition, has a name,
a diagnosis: hoarding.

And what of us, with our pieces
of green sea glass, (not the precious blue),
who can't focus enough
but can't begin to throw out,

caught like the things around us,
ticket stubs, beer coasters, French francs, a few of each.

## Neighbor

I will likely never speak to her
beyond nodding and *Neehao*,
my one word of Mandarin.

We share the language
of being out early
no matter what.

She has a simple jog,
a little faster than a walk.
I have my auburn dog, who pulls.

We nod in all gusts, all degrees.
She wears a gray coat,
sometimes no hat or gloves.

Does her skin register
minute temperature shifts
incrementally like mine?

I think of what I can't
ask her even if I wanted to,
what she might have lived through.

She lives here now,
takes care of baby George,
her son and his wife at work,

doesn't drive, has nowhere to walk to
beyond our peninsula
of shingle and cement,

weather mostly austere.
In a delicate zephyr
I've seen her with George,

hands large and small
batting the leaves
of a white syringa.

**Furnished Model**

Every day he puts up the red and blue balloons
as if he's announcing a child's party

but it's a party of one,
a waiting game.

Who will walk in today and buy?
Who call?

Seeing him attach his balloons to the light pole
I'm not sad for him, but I understand

the daily work routines:
door key, light switch, desk drawer,

the effort to create an atmosphere
in a furnished model home

can wear a person down.
He has to smile. He has to shake your hand or mine

over the blueprints spread across his desk.
No clutter, not even a stray hair.

Anyone who walks in can imagine herself
conversing on the taupe sectional

or pulling the traverse rods
on the checkered window treatments.

No one is walking in.
His silver laptop sleeps among dust motes.

By dusk the balloons have shrunk
like hourglasses

and are drained of color
when he takes them down.

**Adamantine**


The word appeared on the page
from my pen.
I hadn't thought of it or spoken it.

A hard-headedness I kept coming up against
shimmered and beguiled.

Long ago confused
with the Latin *adamare*,

love, attachment,
both lodestone and magnet,

magnet and its opposite,
a legendary stone

of impenetrable hardness,
a diamond's diamond.

The word dared me
as I crawled through indecision.

I know *adamant*, fist on the table,
municipal, insistent,

but *adamantine* sees at night.
It shines in the centuries' dark,

reveals its facets from miles away
and inches from my face,

more anvil than star.
It can crush.

## Thinking of the Anhinga

Beside the sand trap
like a bull fighter's cape
minus the crimson lining,
the anhinga spreads his wings to dry,
black feathers
dramatic, but not beautiful:
a mourning crepe.

It looks uncomfortable
the way he has to hold his wings
up and back
like a child being told
to stand up straight.

Grace in the awkward gesture—

*Walking along on the grass*
*talking at cross purposes.*

Submerged bird, aka
snakebird, water turkey, American darter,
only his long thin beak
juts above the surface, his plumage
not oiled, not waterproof.
Waterlogged, he stays under a long time.

Like a picnic cloth held above the grass
the wings lift
like something about to happen
or that is always happening
or never quite does.

*Falling asleep too early in the evenings.*

They can be found
near standing water, by a canal,
beside a slash pine,
along the Naples city beach.

Severest drought in twenty years,
the fish-eater needs
water to dive into, needs to feed
at Lettuce Lake
in Corkscrew Swamp
with dangerously low
water levels: to find his spot on the bank,
beside the royal ferns, near the moon vine,
the cankerous green pond apples.

*Not doing enough.*
*Doing too much too fast.*

Like the monk in a saffron robe
at the self-serve gas pump,
the anhinga sits and dries his wings.

## Dark Tasks, A Dream

Each night the riderless horse
appears, saddle strapped to his back,
stirrups flying, froth in his mouth,
lips pressed against his teeth.

No way to catch him, grab the reins,
as he careens into the yard
but I know it is my job.
I'm skittish, timid,
lack strength in my arms.
*Don't panic.*

Maternal instinct
tells me he can't be left to roam,
has to be reined in.
And I need
to dodge his kick,
bring him back to the barn.
I have no skills, no gift,
no *way* with a horse.

Where is the hot walker,
horse expert,
to cool him down, curry him,
walk him in the ring?

And the rider?
Is he someone
I've left behind?

Whatever I thought I once knew
how to do I've forgotten.

I try to coax the chestnut,
my palm up, empty.
He snorts and paws the ground.

I wish I knew what to say
to calm him.

I put down my whip,
pull on one boot.

He must be fed, but what?
Nothing picked from the garden,
nothing that can be named.

## Time Travel

International Date Line:
a term learned in school,

dotted line on a map
I thought I would never cross.

Twenty four hours, an entire day away.
Mysterious as the equator

the Line divided day from day
day from night

the arbitrary way
the earth was split in half.

I learned Tuesday could be
Wednesday, a day gained or lost

depending how you traveled
most of a day spent in the air.

East or West.
Geography crossed into Math.

But how did I miss
knowing China has one time zone?

\*

A friend who lives at the equator
tells me days up north

are too long or too short.
Hers are cut neatly in half.

The sun sets at seven
in a reassuring rhythm

as though rowing:
one oar in light, one in the dark.

\*

A country was called Burma or Siam,
old names, when I shaded in the map

with colored pencils.
I'm searching for the simple

street or city, a date in history, syllables
to recite like stones I can hold in my hand

without ambiguity or ambivalence;
*war assassination house arrest*

*pestilence or flood*
become words like artifacts or curiosities.

\*

My son now on the other side
of the International Date Line

revels in conveyances:
taxi, train, plane, motorcycle,

underground, ferry, bicycle, pedicab.
His passport's stamped

more than once a day,
its pages multiply,

visas, customs
he breezes through.

He knows the rules.
He reads the signs:

*Do not wait for anybody.*
*Keep moving.*

## Direction

You would have known exactly what wind
swept across the parking lot this morning:
an engaging wind, not fierce, not the kind
to sting my ears or turn away from, or combat,
to make me rush inside to my appointment.
It bent back the grasses by the railroad tracks
and carried a salt scent from the fields
miles inland from the sea.
I lingered in it, trying to determine
where it was coming from, southeast or west,
and who would have relied on it, or labored in it,
sailor or hunter, tensed to
a gust bringing rain on its back,
caught in a moment's feather-light maelstrom.

## High Summer

I kept thinking of the phrase
as I walked, its transience, a trick

that lets me step outside
barefoot in light cotton

next to nothing
between indoors and out.

Did I come upon it
or did it envelope me?

A high point, a musical note
that holds.

A state or measure of time?
Time outside of time.

Some creatures estivate:
doze out the days

in their carapaces.
I am emboldened

egged on, reckless
ready to surrender,

up outside all night
elated. Anticipation

is another kind of carapace
as if I could breathe

underwater, forget it ends
as it begins.

Helena Minton has published *Personal Effects* and *The Canal Bed* with Alice James Books, and *The Gardener and the Bees* with March Street Press. Her poems have appeared in a variety of journals, including *Poetry, The Beloit Poetry Journal, Sou'wester,* and *West Branch.* Poems have also been anthologized in *Raising Lilly Ledbetter: Women Poets Occupy the Workspace, Sojourner: A Feminist Anthology,* and *Merrimack: A Poetry Anthology.*

She has taught English Composition and Creative Writing and worked for many years as a public librarian. She has an MFA in Creative Writing from the University of Massachusetts/Amherst and serves on the Board of the Robert Frost Foundation, in Lawrence, Massachusetts. She lives north of Boston.

www.ingramcontent.com/pod-product-compliance
Lightning Source LLC
LaVergne TN
LVHW041509070426
835507LV00012B/1440